Violin I

SCHIRMER'S LIBRARY
OF MUSICAL CLASSICS

F. MAZAS

Duets
For Two Violins

Op. 38   **Twelve Little Duets**
(Edited and Fingered by HENRY SCHRADIECK)

   → Book I   —   Library Vol. 331   —
        Book II   —   Library Vol. 332   —

Op. 39   **Six Duets**
(Edited and Fingered by HENRY SCHRADIECK)

        Book I   —   Library Vol. 333   —
        Book II   —   Library Vol. 334   —

Op. 46   **Six Little Duets**
(Edited and Fingered by PHILIPP MITTELL)

    Library Vol. 1250   —   —   —

Op. 70   **Twelve Little Duets**
(Edited and Fingered by FRIEDRICH HERMANN)

        Book I   —   Library Vol. 446   —
        Book II   —   Library Vol. 447   —

G. SCHIRMER, Inc.

DISTRIBUTED BY
HAL•LEONARD®
7777 W. BLUEMOUND RD. P.O. BOX 13819 MILWAUKEE, WI 53213

Twelve little Duets.

Down – bow ⊓.
Up – bow V.

VIOLIN I.

F. Mazas. Op. 38, Book I.

Allegro maestoso.

1.

ROMANCE.
Andante.

VIOLIN I.

RONDO.
Allegro.

VIOLIN I.

Allegro moderato.

2.

VIOLIN I.

RONDO.
Allegretto.

VIOLIN I.

3. Allegro.

A

ROMANCE.
Andante.

VIOLIN I.

RONDO.
Allegretto.

VIOLIN I.

VIOLIN I.

RONDO.
Allegretto.

VIOLIN I.

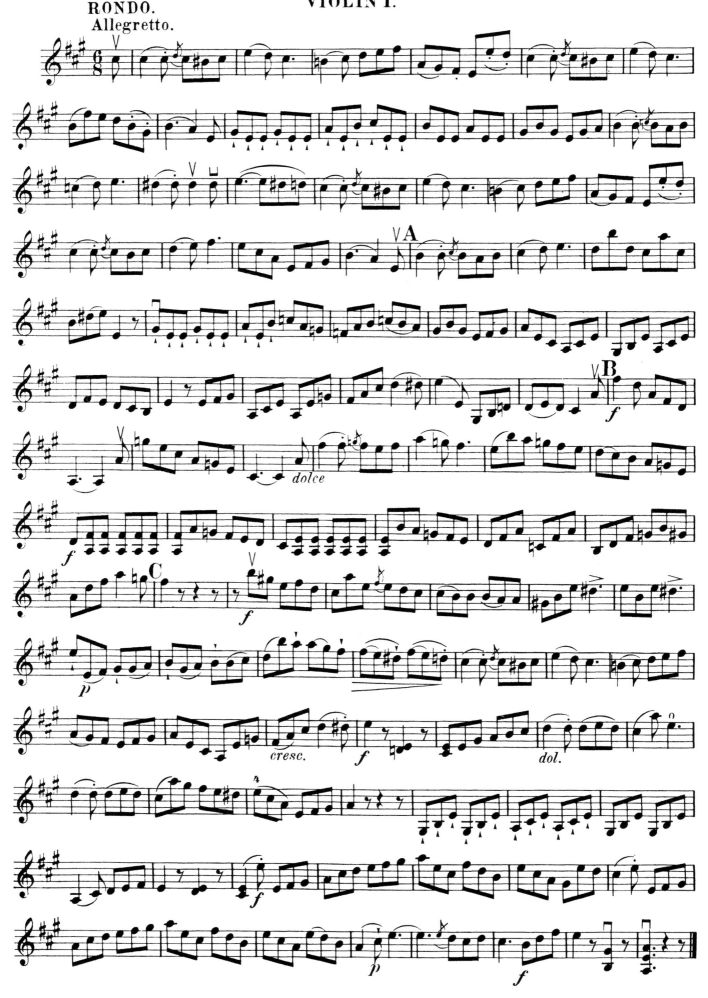

VIOLIN I.

Tempo di Marcia.

RONDO.
Allegretto.

VIOLIN I.

VIOLIN I.

VIOLIN I.

RONDO,
Allegretto.

Violin II

SCHIRMER'S LIBRARY
OF MUSICAL CLASSICS

F. MAZAS

Duets

For Two Violins

G. SCHIRMER, Inc.

DISTRIBUTED BY
HAL•LEONARD®
CORPORATION
7777 W. BLUEMOUND RD. P.O. BOX 13819 MILWAUKEE, WI 53213

Twelve little Duets.

Down-bow ⊓.
Up-bow V.

VIOLIN II.

F. Mazas. Op.38, Book I.

VIOLIN II.

VIOLIN II.

VIOLIN II.

VIOLIN II.

VIOLIN II.

VIOLIN II.

RONDO.
Allegretto.

Allegro moderato.

5.

VIOLIN II.

VIOLIN II.

VIOLIN II.

VIOLIN II.

Andante non troppo lento.

VIOLIN II.